# Rookie
## Read-About® Math

# Math Tools

WITHDRAWN

## By Melanie Chrismer

**Consultants**
Chalice Bennett
Elementary Specialist
Martin Luther King Jr. Laboratory School
Evanston, Illinois

Ari Ginsburg
Math Curriculum Specialist

Children's Press®
A Division of Scholastic Inc.
New York   Toronto   London   Auckland   Sydney
Mexico City   New Delhi   Hong Kong
Danbury, Connecticut

W9-CDM-922

Designer: Herman Adler Design
Photo Researcher: Caroline Anderson
The photo on the cover shows peppers on a scale.

**Library of Congress Cataloging-in-Publication Data**

Chrismer, Melanie.
  Math tools / by Melanie Chrismer.
     p. cm. — (Rookie read-about math)
  ISBN 0-516-24961-4 (lib. bdg.)    0-516-25550-9 (pbk.)
  1. Measuring instruments—Juvenile literature. I. Title. II. Series.
  QC100.5.C47 2006
  681'.2—dc22
                                    2005019972

© 2006 by Scholastic Inc.
All rights reserved. Published simultaneously in Canada.
Printed in Mexico.

CHILDREN'S PRESS, and ROOKIE READ-ABOUT®,
and associated logos are trademarks and/or registered trademarks
of Scholastic Library Publishing. SCHOLASTIC and associated logos
are trademarks and/or registered trademarks of Scholastic Inc.

1 2 3 4 5 6 7 8 9 10 R 15 14 13 12 11 10 09 08 07 06

It's hard to measure things
with a foot-long hot dog.
Use a math tool instead.

There are many math tools.

Math tools help you measure and count.

Math tools make math easier.

A ruler is a math tool.

A ruler measures how long something is.

A ruler measures length.

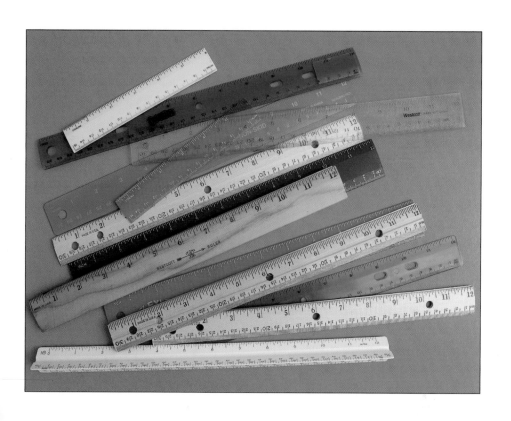

Some rulers measure in
inches. There are 12 inches
in 1 foot.

Rulers are great.

A ruler cannot measure
the amount of milk inside
a glass.

A measuring cup can.

A measuring cup is a math tool.

Measuring cups measure the space taken up by a liquid or anything that can be poured.

Measuring cups measure volume (VOL-yuhm).

Some measuring cups measure in ounces. There are 8 ounces in 1 cup.

Measuring cups are great.

A measuring cup cannot
tell you if you have a fever.

A thermometer
(thur-MOM-uh-tur) can.

A thermometer is a math tool.

A thermometer tells you how hot or cold something is.

A thermometer measures temperature (TEM-pur-uh-chur).

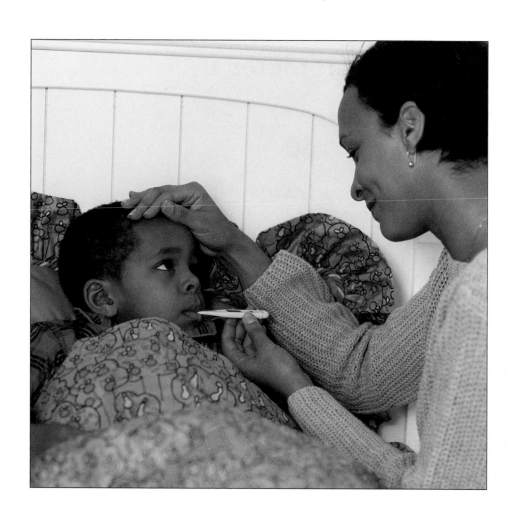

This thermometer shows that the weather is warm.

Thermometers measure
temperature in degrees.
A higher degree number
means a hotter temperature.

Thermometers are great.

A thermometer cannot
tell you if you are on
time for school.

A clock can.

A clock is a math tool.

A clock tells you what time it is.

A clock counts time.

20

A clock counts in seconds, minutes, and hours. The hands on a clock point to the time.

Clocks are great.

A clock cannot tell you how many days there are until your birthday.

A calendar can.

A calendar is a math tool.

A calendar shows the order of days. It shows past days, today, and future days.

A calendar shows the days, weeks, and months of the year.

23

Calendars are great.

A calendar can tell you when your birthday is coming.

It cannot tell you that you weigh more than you did last year.

A scale can.

A scale is a math tool.

A scale tells you how heavy something is.

A scale measures weight.

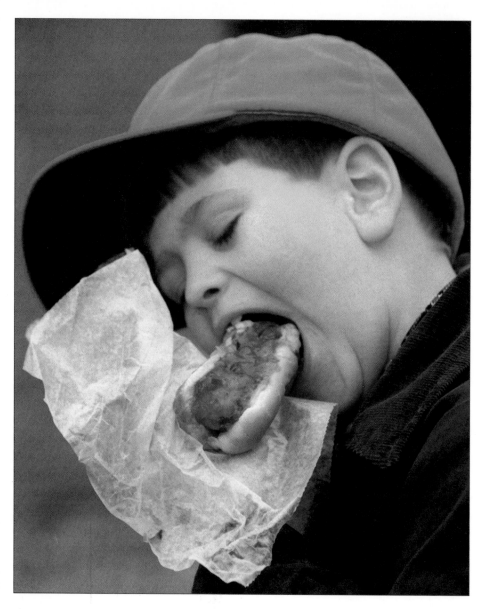

Foot-long hot dogs are great to eat.

Math tools are great for counting and measuring.

# Words You Know

calendar

clock

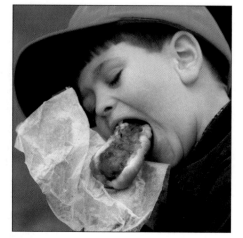

hot dog

measure

30

measuring cup

ruler

scale

thermometer

31

# Index

# About the Author

Melanie Chrismer is a writer and flutist who lives near Atlanta, Georgia. She loves reading, writing, and eating foot-long hot dogs with lots of mustard.

# Photo Credits

Photographs ©2006: Corbis Images: 5 top left (Laura Dwight), 27, 31 bottom left (C. Lyttle/zefa), 15 (Ariel Skelley); ImageState: 24 (Rubberball Productions), 20, 30 top right (Joe Sohm/VisionsofAmerica.com); PhotoEdit: 6, 23, 30 top left, 31 top right (Richard Hutchings), 12, 31 top left (Felicia Martinez), 5 bottom right, 19 (Michael Newman), 11 (Michael Ventura), 3, 5 bottom left, 5 top right, 30 bottom right (David Young-Wolff); Superstock, Inc./Yoshi Tomii: cover; The Image Works: 16, 31 bottom right (Bob Daemmrich), 8 (Ellen B. Senisi), 28, 30 bottom left (Steve Warmowski/Journal-Courier).